DYNAMIC STUDIES IN JAMES

Bringing God's Word to Life

FRED A. SCHEEREN

WestBow Press
A DIVISION OF THOMAS NELSON
& ZONDERVAN

WestBow Press books may be ordered through booksellers or by contacting:

WestBow Press
A Division of Thomas Nelson & Zondervan
1663 Liberty Drive
Bloomington, IN 47403
www.westbowpress.com
1 (866) 928-1240

Because of the dynamic nature of the Internet, any web addresses or links contained in this book may have changed since publication and may no longer be valid. The views expressed in this work are solely those of the author and do not necessarily reflect the views of the publisher, and the publisher hereby disclaims any responsibility for them.

Any people depicted in stock imagery provided by Thinkstock are models, and such images are being used for illustrative purposes only.
Certain stock imagery © Thinkstock.

ISBN: 978-1-4908-4909-6 (sc)
ISBN: 978-1-4908-4910-2 (e)

Library of Congress Control Number: 2014915343

Printed in the United States of America.

WestBow Press rev. date: 09/22/2014

DEDICATION

I DEDICATE THIS book to my lovely wife, Sally, who is a Jewish believer. She has stood by me over the years and raised our sons in a God-loving home. The comfort of sharing our friendship and love for Christ has encouraged me greatly in creating this series of dynamic studies of various books of the Bible. Sally's participation in our small group studies has added a much deeper dimension of richness to the discussions. Thank you for sharing your heritage, training, and knowledge.

CONTENTS

PREFACE

WELCOME TO WHAT I hope you'll find to be a most enjoyable study of the book of James, part of the Judeo-Christian documents which we call the Bible. Many believers claim James as their favorite body of Scripture because of its practical application to everyday life.

As we consider how this book fits into the whole of the New Testament documents and the Tanakh (the name used for the Old Testament by Jews, is used here to emphasize the Jewishness of the Scriptures), we need to realize a number of things. We need to stand in awe of this collection of 66 books, written over thousands of years by at least 40 different authors. Every detail of the text is there by design. It explains history before it happens, and comes to us from outside the dimension of time. It is, in short, the most amazing, most authenticated, and most accurate book available in the world.

If this claim is not strong enough, add to it the indisputable fact that the words contained therein have changed more lives than any others now in existence.

And now back to this particular study.

I intended this particular study to be used in a small group setting; however, it can also be adapted to a larger group or individual study.

While the subject of our study, the Judeo-Christian Scriptures, are demonstrably perfect, my prepared studies are not. There is no way that I, or anyone else, could possibly incorporate the depth of the text into individual sessions. I simply desire to provide a vehicle for others to use in their investigation of the Scriptures as they incorporate these timeless truths into their lives.

One perfect example of the depth of Scripture and the impossibility of capturing that depth all at one time comes from an interesting experience I had when putting similar sessions together on the book of Romans. One Saturday morning I was trying to prepare several sessions in one sitting. By the time I finished the third session, I was mentally exhausted. About a month later, when it came time to present the third session, I forgot that I had already prepared it. So I spent two more hours getting the study ready again. When I realized my mistake, I compared the two sessions and was surprised to find that they were very different. One person, studying the same material, utilizing the same resources, got two very different lessons out of it. This will happen time and again as we continue to plumb the depths of the Word of God.

ACKNOWLEDGEMENTS

MY FRIEND, BOB Mason, who at the time of this writing was in his second career as the Pastor of Small Groups at the Bible Chapel in the South Hills of Pittsburgh, suggested the overall structure of each study session. Realizing that our group was doing more in-depth work than most, he asked that I include several important segments in each session; most specifically, the warm-up phase and the life application phase.

One great resource for this, suggested by Bob, is the New Testament Lesson Planner from InterVarsity Press. I have augmented this with commentaries by Chuck Missler from Koinonia House, as well as the whole of Scripture itself. In order to make the utilization of the whole of Scripture more efficient, I have also leaned heavily on the Libronix Digital Library, perhaps the most advanced Bible software available. I have also utilized a number of other resources to help us understand how the New Testament and the Tanakh fit together as one cohesive document.

Dr. David Fink helped make preparing this material easier by periodically sending me scriptural cross-references. David continues to send me cross-references for any chapter of the Scriptures in question so that I can weave them into the discussion as appropriate.

Finally, I would like to acknowledge the members of our small group Bible study, with whom I first reviewed and utilized this material. This fine group of diverse people has grown closer together as a result of our regular meetings and we have seen some miraculous things happen in each other's lives. Our members include:

- Dan Chunko, a criminal attorney who also plays keyboards for the Bible Chapel (Dan is the only person I know who can play three keyboards at one time…)

- Alison Chunko, a business owner who was healed of a deadly lung disease during the course of our studies

- Cathy Harvey, a high school teacher and dog breeder who was also healed of a serious eye disorder during the course of our studies

- Dr. David Fink, a former pastor and professor of Greek

- Joyce Smith Fink, former assistant to the President at Pittsburgh Theological Seminary

- Scott Swart, former marine with a White House security clearance and currently involved with the Washington City Mission

- Wendy Swart, a business owner and operator

- Ron Carrola, a well-known transportation engineer

- Felicia Carrola, who is fully engaged homeschooling her several children, one of whom is composing full orchestral scores while still in high school

- Tom Nicastro, the local service manager for a major international corporation

- Cindy Nicastro, a physical therapist with many years of expertise and experience

- My wife Sally, an attorney in private practice, whose Jewish brother, a successful real estate developer, became a believer during the course of our studies in the book of Romans

I thank you all.

Of course, having read the roster of the people in this particular small group, you may be wondering how you could *not* have a great Bible study with so many well-read, intelligent, and successful people in it. The mix of people, of course, is no accident. God's plan is greater than any we can imagine, and His caring for us certainly includes the makeup of any small group devoted to the study of His Word. I believe that every such small group convened for this purpose will have a mix of participants similarly suited to enhance the growth and learning of the group members individually and the group as a whole.

I believe you will find going through this material enjoyable and helpful. You will likely find it even more enjoyable if you have the privilege of going through it with a small group of believers such as I have been privileged to do. I know I have enjoyed going through these studies and feel as though I have gotten more out of the experience than I would have if I had only engaged in the study by myself.

Speaking of small groups, Dr. Chuck Missler, a former Fortune 500 CEO, claims that this is where he experienced the greatest growth in his life as a believer. I believe that you may find this to be true in your experience and encourage you to be an active participant in such a mutually supportive, biblically-based group.

May God bless you, inspire you, teach you, and change your life for the better as you go through these sessions.

INTRODUCTION
GROUND RULES

I DESIGNED THE first portion of each study to encourage everyone to think about their personal situation and get them involved. I designed the second portion to help people understand what the text says and how it relates to the whole of Scripture. And finally, each session ends with a discussion designed to help those present apply that day's lesson to their lives.

You will notice that in most instances I have included the citation, but not the actual text of the portion of Scripture that we are considering. This is on purpose. I believe we all learn more effectively if we have to dig out the text for ourselves. As a byproduct of that exercise, we all become more familiar with this marvelous book.

You will also notice that the Scripture references are preceded or followed by a question, or series of questions. Again, this is on purpose. I have also found that people seem to learn most effectively when employing the "Socratic Method." That is, instead of telling someone what the text says and how it relates to other texts and life, they will remember it much more completely if they answer questions about it and ferret the information out for themselves.

In a few instances, I have inserted additional commentary or partial answers to some of the questions to help the group get the greatest possible good out of the study.

In addition, I have added various scriptural references, intending that they be read out loud as part of the session. Shorter passages might be read by one participant, while anything over two or three verses might serve everyone better if one member reads one verse and another reads the next until the passage is completed. This keeps everyone involved. After reading these passages, I intend that they be seriously considered as they relate to the primary Scripture at hand in James. At times, this relationship seems to be available and obvious on the surface. In many other instances, the interconnectedness of the whole of Scripture and its principles are most effectively understood through deeper thought, discussion, and prayer along the way.

In commenting on and discussing the various scriptures, questions, concepts, and principles in this material, it is not required that any particular person give their input. The reader of any passage may, but is not required, to give their thoughts to the group. This is a group participation exercise for the mutual benefit of all involved and many people in the group giving their insight into a certain passage or question will often enhance the learning experience.

I also have two very practical suggestions if you do this in a small group setting. Every time you meet, I suggest you review the calendar and go over meetings scheduled for the future and who will be bringing refreshments. This just makes things run a lot better while enhancing everyone's enjoyment and expectations.

BRIEF BACKGROUND TO THE BOOK OF JAMES

THE BOOK OF James appears to have been written no later than 62 A.D., 62 years after the birth of Christ, and no more than 30 years after His death and resurrection.

If you are fifty years of age or more and you think back to what happened thirty years ago, it seems very fresh in your memory. This was the case for James and his readers at the time. Everything was fresh and real. They had absolutely no logical reason to doubt about what so many of them had seen, heard, and touched. Imagine shaking hands with Jesus Christ.

In this book, we find at least sixty imperatives in only 108 verses. The Fourth Edition of the Houghton Mifflin Harcourt American Heritage Dictionary, copyrighted and updated in 2008 defines an imperative in its' electronic edition for Smart Phones as "a command, an order, an obligation, a duty, a rule, a principle, or instinct that compels a certain behavior." We find more such guidance in this very short book than in any other book of the New Testament.

For this reason, many believers find James to be their favorite book in the whole of the Bible.

It is true that God gave us this book and the whole of his Word because He loves us. However, the fact that he needed to spell things out so clearly in this book is no great compliment to those to whom it was written, or to us.

More than anything else, the fact that God needed to give us this book through James proves our depravity without Him. A number of years ago Mahatma Ghandi, a very famous leader in India, was asked what he saw as the greatest barrier to Christianity in India. He replied in one word: "Christians."

The way we behave toward people reveals how we feel about God and speaks volumes about our relationship with God.

James draws us back to the reality of our relationship with God and the supremacy of His Word.

He repeats in real terms of everyday life and action what we find throughout the Scriptures. He reminds us of our responsibilities and what must happen in our lives to accomplish our calling.

Through the centuries, many people have said that the book of James contradicts the book of Romans.

Nothing could be further from the truth. God has given us this important portion of His Word so our lives might more fully reflect His nature. The principles James reiterates in this book can also be gleaned elsewhere in the Bible. Having them all in one place, where they keep hitting you in the face, makes some people very uncomfortable.

Of course, we need to study James if we want to better understand and experience the positive transformation of our minds and lives, not to mention the new hearts that God offers to us.

The following scriptures from the Old and New Testament help set the stage for what God communicates to us in the book of James.

- Matthew 7:14

  14 But the gateway to life is small, and the road is narrow, and only a few ever find it.

- Ephesians 5:15-16

  15 So be careful how you live, not as fools but as those who are wise.

  16 Make the most of every opportunity for doing good in these evil days.

- Philippians 2:13-16

  13 For God is working in you, giving you the desire to obey him and the power to do what pleases him.

  14 In everything you do, stay away from complaining and arguing,

  15 so that no one can speak a word of blame against you. You are to live clean, innocent lives as children of God in a dark world full of crooked and perverse people. Let your lives shine brightly before them.

  16 Hold tightly to the word of life, so that when Christ returns, I will be proud that I did not lose the race and that my work was not useless.

- Daniel 12:3

  3 Those who are wise will shine as bright as the sky, and those who lead many to righteousness will shine like the stars forever.

- Psalm 94:12

  12 Happy are those whom you discipline, Lord, and those whom you teach from your law.

- Revelation 3:19

  19 I correct and discipline everyone I love. So be diligent and turn from your indifference.

DEVELOPING ENDURANCE AND MAKING A DIFFERENCE

JAMES 1:1-18

Opening Prayer

Group Warm-up Question

As we lead into our study of James itself, let's discuss how we feel about the following statement: "Your results in life are determined 10% by what happens to you and 90% by how you respond to it."

Read James 1:1-18 one verse at a time.

To whom in particular is this letter written?

Why did he refer to this group as he did? (See the NLT for help with this.)

How do we refer to this group today—in our language, in our culture, and as it relates to the long-term plan of God?

Read James 1:1-4 again and feel free to comment.

Read and comment on the following verses:

   Matthew 5:10-12

   1 Peter 1:6-7

   James 1:12

   Revelation 3:19

   Romans 5:2-5

What attitude did James say we should exhibit in the midst of trials?

Why must we make a very conscious and deliberate decision about how to respond when we are faced with problems and trials in life? (Remember that in human cognition, every emotion is preceded by a thought, even when we are not aware of it.)

Let's list some of the positive results of testing, trials, and tribulations.

1.

2.

3.

4.

5.

6.

7.

8.

9.

10.

Read James 1:5-8 one verse at a time.

What promise do we find in these verses?

What do we find out about the source of the fulfillment of this promise in Proverbs 1:7?

How does this work in our lives in real time?

What accompanying warning do we also find?

Read and comment on the following verses:

Hebrews 11:6

Jeremiah 29:11-13

James 1:8

Is it possible that being double-minded, or having the characteristic of being constantly changeable, shows an inflated ego or an unsubdued mind? Why or why not?

Read and comment on the following verses:

Psalm 25:9

Matthew 7:7-8

What preconditions does Jesus presume in these two verses?

Read James 1:9-11 one verse at a time.

Why do you think these verses say what they do about our achievements in the same breath as monetary riches? (Note: All wealth is relative. One person can have $10 million and believe he or she is rich. The next person can have the same amount and believe that he or she is poor.)

How does the way in which we view ourselves and our relationship to God determine if we see ourselves as rich in monetary terms, regardless of the balance in our bank account?

Jesus commented on the problem of improperly viewing and using material possessions. His disciples thought this concept so important that the same recounting of one of His statements about the subject appears in three of the four Gospels.

See the following verses:

Luke 18:25

Matthew 19:24

Mark 10:25

Why did this make such an impression upon Matthew, Luke, and Mark?

Note: In the time Jesus walked the earth, towns were surrounded by walls to keep out marauders. When the gates to the city were closed be it day or night, it was almost impossible for someone to get into town on a camel. However, they could do so through an opening called a "needle," a low doorway into the city that a camel could traverse by getting down on its knees and gradually shuffling its way through the gate. It was very difficult, but it could be done. This prevented a group of armed bandits from riding right into the city.

What eventually happens to the monetary riches we have accumulated?

Read Psalm 39:4-7 one verse at a time and comment.

In what way do material riches and possessions disappoint people once they possess them?

Which of the things we have achieved or done in life really matter?

Read and comment on the following verses:

    1 Corinthians 3:13-15

    2 Peter 3:10-11

Read Psalm 90:12.

How does this verse sum up the concepts of our wealth, how we use it, and how we live?

Reread James 1:13-18 one verse at a time.

What is the significance of the way the word "wants" is used in verse 13? (We may need to look at the NLT as we discuss this.)

Read and comment on the following verses:

Psalm 7:14

Ezekiel 18:4

Ezekiel 18:24 (shudder)

It has been said that the biggest danger is not what is being done *to* us, but what is being done *by* us. How do you feel about this statement?

Therefore, is it then more important to pray "Lord, keep me pure," rather than "Lord, keep me safe"? (Note: David, who was often under attack, seemed to think so.)

Read what he had to say about this in Psalm 25:4-5, 20-21 one verse at a time. Please feel free to comment.

Read Luke 11:9-13 one verse at a time and comment.

What, then, is the source of the good things we experience in life?

What particularly important gift do we find ourselves the recipient of in James 1:18?

Application Question

What do you think God wants to teach you this week through the things you're dealing with in your life?

Close in Prayer.

Review Calendar.

Assign Refreshments for next time.

SUCCESSFUL LIVING AND GOD'S PERFECT LAW

JAMES 1:19-27

Opening Prayer

Group Warm-up Question

Who do you admire as a religious or spiritual role model?

Read James 1:19-27 one verse at a time.

In the first 18 verses of James we learned about the benefits we accrue as we go through difficult times. Some people say that verses 19-27 give us appropriate ways to deal with such situations. How do you feel about this statement?

Read James 1:19 again.

What secrets about human communication do we learn in this verse?

Read the following verses to see what else the Scriptures tell us about these secrets.

Proverbs 14:29

Proverbs 15:18

Proverbs 16:32

Proverbs 19:11

Is this easy to do?

Have you ever had an experience where you were on the verge of acting in a nonproductive fashion when your knowledge of the Scriptures, along with the Holy Spirit, helped you respond differently?

Read James 1:20 again.

What is the problem with our anger?

How do you reconcile the concept of the human emotion of anger with the emotion you see God expressing throughout the Scriptures, or with what you sometimes see Jesus Christ express in the books written by Matthew, Mark, Luke, and John?

What does the anger we sometimes see from God tell us about His character?

How do you relate Matthew 5:21-22 to anger and speech in our lives? Read this in the KJV for the greatest clarity.

Read Ephesians 4:26 and comment.

When is our anger appropriate and what should be the result?

Read and comment on the following verses:

1 Kings 10:9

2 Chronicles 9:8

Psalm 33:5

Psalm 89:14

Psalm 106:3

Isaiah 56:1

Jeremiah 22:3

Hosea 12:6

Proverbs 21:3

Amos 5:15

James 1:21-22

What did James say should not be in the life of a believer?

Why did James need to say this?

James says that if we listen to God's Word but don't obey, we fool ourselves. Can we actually fool ourselves?

How does this happen, and what are the results?

Read Matthew 7:22-23 and comment.

Does this imply that a person can fool themselves and others to the point of destruction?

How should we respond to this possibility?

Read John 17:17 to see if this helps our understanding.

Read James 1:23-24 again.

Also read 1 Corinthians 13:12.

The reference here to mirrors is an interesting one from an historical point. The best mirrors of that time in history were made from Corinthian bronze. However, all mirrors from that period were of poor quality compared to the accurate reflections in the mirrors of today. Mirrors were an expensive and uncommon luxury. A person could indeed forget what they looked like since they did not often have a mirror at hand. Think about just how common mirrors are today, and how often we use them. Can you imagine what life today would be like without mirrors?

What point does James make with this mirror analogy?

Read James 1:25 again.

What vitally important positive promise from God do we find in this passage?

How would you describe the necessary preconditions to receiving the benefits of this promise?

Read John 8:31-32 and explain how this fits together with what we just read in James 1:25

What other factor in this process do we observe in 1 John 1:9?

Some have said that for forgiveness to be complete there must also be repentance. Repentance involves a changing of the way. How do you think James would have responded to this?

Reread James 1:25 and dissect the four components of becoming a doer of God's Word.

1. Looking intently into God's Word

2. Continuing to look, and doing so regularly, on a daily basis

3. Remembering His Word

4. Doing what His Word says

Read James 1:26 again and comment.

Note: The Greek word used here for bridling or controlling one's tongue is *chalinagogeo*, which means "to bridle, hold in check, restrain, keep a tight rein on." What insight does this give us into what God tells us in this verse?

Note: Here again, in the same brief passage, we have James warning us against fooling ourselves. Let's read some other verses to see how James relates this to the tongue.

Read and comment on the following verses:

James 2:12

James 3:1-3

James 3:14-18

James 4:11-12

Matthew 12:34-35

Note: God tells us that we have a responsibility to help the oppressed. Let's see what we learn about this in the following verses.

James 1:27

Exodus 22:20-24

Psalm 146:9

Isaiah 1:17

Romans 12:1-2

How important are these concepts as we live out our lives?

Application Question

In what situations do you need to be particularly careful to be sure that your words and actions reflect the change God has made (and continues to make) in you?

Close in prayer

Review calendar.

Assign refreshments for next time.

EVALUATION BASED UPON REALITY (TRUE RICHES)

JAMES 2:1-13

Opening Prayer

Group Warm-up Question

How much money would it take for you to consider yourself rich?

Read James 2:1-13 one verse at a time.

Note: Roman law at the time favored the rich. Persons of lower class cold not initiate lawsuits against someone from a higher class. In addition, the law prescribed harsher penalties for those of a lower class than those of a higher class.

Note: Jews in the time of Jesus also coveted recognition and honor and competed rigorously with one another for praise.

Read Luke 14:7-14 to see this in action.

Does this same situation exist today for both Jews and Gentiles?

Do you think this is part of an unregenerate human nature?

How did Jesus Christ treat people in terms of their wealth or status?

Read Matthew 22:16 and comment.

Was this a new idea in Scripture?

Read and comment on the following verses:
    Deuteronomy 16:19
    1 Samuel 2:1-10

1 Corinthians 1:26-27

Leviticus 19:15

Note: Jewish legal texts, written in contemplation of the Scriptures, condemned judges who permitted one litigant to stand while the other was permitted to sit. To avoid partiality based upon clothing, some second century rabbis required both litigants to dress in the same kind of clothes.

Is it possible to be rich in this world and poor in the next, or poor in this world and rich in the next (judging by human measures of wealth alone)?

Read Proverbs 30:8 and comment.

Why do you think that Solomon, the most financially prosperous man in the history of the world, would write something like this?

The passage we are considering today in James speaks of monetary riches. However, in our society, other things are often accorded the same type of recognition. Consider the following:

1. Athletic ability and accomplishment

2. Organizational status

3. Elected officials

4. Other life accomplishments

Do you think these same concepts from James apply to the short list above? If they do, how should a believer live in regard to them?

Read and comment on the following verses:

1 Timothy 6:17-18

1 Peter 1:17-19

Note: Rudyard Kipling wrote an interesting poem entitled "If." It does not carry the same weight as Scripture, though interestingly it does embody some scriptural principles. In particular, it speaks about treating the "imposters of success and failure the same." Take a look at this poem and see what you think about this concept. The poem is included at the end of this week's study.

James 2:8 and James 2:12 speak of the law of love. Read these verses again.

Note: A royal law was an imperial edict and carried a great deal of weight at the time. How much more weight, then, does an edict given by the King of kings carry?

How have some people misused James 2:8 and James 2:12 when taking them out of context?

What is the correct use of these verses in relationship to the whole of Scripture?

Read and comment on the following verses:

Leviticus 19:18

John 13:34

Romans 5:5

1 Thessalonians 4:9

Romans 13:10

Note: It is important that we apply God's standards as revealed to us in the whole of Scripture to fully understand this concept.

Read and comment on the following verses:

Hebrews 1:1-3

Hebrews 1:8-9

James 2:10-11

What important constant scriptural concepts do we see reiterated here?

Read James 1:12-13 again and comment.

Why do so many people feel uncomfortable with the concept of being judged?

Let's look at a few other scriptures to see just what this means.

Read and comment on the following verses:

John 5:24

Romans 8:1

Note: These verses bring great comfort to many. However, they do not tell the whole story.

Read and comment on the following verses:

Matthew 12:36

Matthew 5:21-22

Matthew 7:1-5

Matthew 7:21-23

2 Corinthians 5:9-10

Colossians 3:22-25

Psalm 119:41-45

John 14:15-16

Note: Jewish teachers generally defined God's character by two attributes in particular: justice and mercy. They were much more fond of the mercy.

Read Matthew 18:21-35.

How do you see the concepts of justice and mercy working together in this passage?

Application Question

Do you need to change the way you view wealth this week so that it matches the values reflected in the Scriptures?

Close in prayer.

Review calendar.

Assign refreshments for next time.

If

If you can keep your head when all about you

Are losing theirs and blaming it on you;

If you can trust yourself when all men doubt you,

But make allowance for their doubting too;

If you can wait and not be tired by waiting,

Or, being lied about, don't deal in lies,

Or, being hated, don't give way to hating,

And yet don't look too good, nor talk too wise;

If you can dream - and not make dreams your master;

If you can think - and not make thoughts your aim;

If you can meet with triumph and disaster

And treat those two imposters just the same;

If you can bear to hear the truth you've spoken

Twisted by knaves to make a trap for fools,

Or watch the things you gave your life to broken,

And stoop and build 'em up with worn out tools;

If you can make one heap of all your winnings

And risk it on one turn of pitch-and-toss,

And lose, and start again at your beginnings

And never breath a word about your loss;

If you can force your heart and nerve and sinew

To serve your turn long after they are gone,

And so hold on when there is nothing in you

Except the Will which says to them: "Hold on";

If you can talk with crowds and keep your virtue,

Or walk with kings - nor lose the common touch;

If neither foes nor loving friends can hurt you;

If all men count with you, but none too much;

If you can fill the unforgiving minute

With sixty seconds' worth of distance run -

Yours is the Earth and everything that's in it,

And—which is more—you'll be a Man my son!

NO GUTS, NO GLORY OR NO DEEDS, NO FAITH

JAMES 2:14-26

Opening Prayer

Group Warm-up Question

What do you see as the difference between someone who talks about a problem and someone who does something about it?

Most people talk about the centrality of faith and God's grace as we see it in the following verses:

Ephesians 2:8-9

2 Corinthians 5:7

Hebrews 11:6

Romans 14:23

However, James 2:14-26 reminds us that this must be understood in the context of the whole of Scripture to be effective in our lives.

This vital passage helps us to understand the true nature of faith and to live victorious lives as Christians. Chuck Missler said that "Faith is not believing just because of the evidence for our faith and the veracity of the Judeo-Christian Scriptures, but also obeying in spite of the consequences."[1] Remember, the evidence is incontrovertible. Our obedience should also be such that it has the same ring of truth to those who carefully observe how we live on a day-to-day basis.

Larry Norman—popularly known as the Father of Christian Rock in such wide-ranging places including *Christianity Today*, *National Public Radio*, *CNN*, *The New York Times*, and *Wikipedia*—put it more bluntly when he said, "Be a real Christian, baby. Don't be a jerk."

How do you feel about these two statements by Chuck Missler and Larry Norman?

What is wrong with having faith without deeds?

James 2:14-26 points us to three distinct kinds of faith: demonic faith, dead faith, and dynamic faith.

Demonic Faith

Read:

Mark 3:11-12

Mark 5:1-13

James 2:19

Dead Faith

Read:

Matthew 7:21

James 2:14

James 2:17

James 2:20

Note: The Greek word for "dead" in James 2:20 means barren or idle, as in money that is drawing no interest.

What can we infer from understanding this nuance of meaning from the Greek?

Read:

> James 2:26
>
> Titus 1:16

Dynamic Faith

Read:

> Galatians 6:10
>
> Matthew 25:40
>
> Galatians 5:6
>
> 1 John 3:17-18

James also cites Abraham in his discussion about faith.

Read:

> James 2:21-23
>
> Genesis 15:5-6

According to these scriptures, how do we know that Abraham's faith was real and effective?

Note: The verb in Greek for the phrase "was made complete" found in James 2:22 is *eteleiothe* which comes from *teleioo*. This means "made complete," and the word "faith" in direct connection with "works" infers that faith without actions is simply useless and does not count at all. This is the one place in the

New Testament where we find this direct connection in the Greek so it is of great significance. The principle is stated elsewhere in different ways, but is the most clear in this passage.

Read:

Romans 4:1-5

Galatians 3:6-7

What important characteristics of Abraham's faith made it full and complete?

Jesus also had some other things to say about faith. How might we summarize what he said in the following verses?

Matthew 7:12-20

Matthew 12:33-37

Luke 10:25-37

John Calvin said "It is faith alone that justifies, but faith that justifies is never alone." How do you feel about his statement?

Hebrews 11:1-26 is often called the "Hall of Faith." Perhaps it might also be called "The Hall of Works." What do we learn as we read this passage?

According to James 2:24, how is a person made right with God?

CHARACTERISTICS OF DYNAMIC AND EFFECTIVE SAVING FAITH

Faith is only as good as its object. Read 1 John 5:12.

Dynamic faith is based upon the word of God.

Read:

    James 1:18

    James 1:21

    Romans 10:17

Dynamic faith involves the whole person.

Dynamic faith always leads to action.

How should being a follower of Jesus Christ change the way we live?

Dead faith produces certain types of things in the lives of people. List as many as you can.

Conversely, a living dynamic faith also produces certain unmistakable things in the lives of people. List as many as you can think of.

Read Galatians 5:19-24 for an overall perspective on this.

Finally, and most importantly, read 2 Corinthians 13:5.

Answer the most important question of your life. Do you pass this test?

Application Question

How can you show your faith in God and demonstrate that you have true life in Jesus Christ by what you do this coming week?

Close in prayer

Review calendar.

Assign refreshments for next time.

LOOSE LIPS SINK SHIPS AND LIVES

JAMES 3:1-12

Opening prayer

Group Warm-up Question

What can you learn about a person by listening to them speak

Read James 3:1-12.

What kinds of things can motivate a person to become a teacher?

What particular responsibilities does a teacher have when that teacher is a believer?

Why will God judge teachers more strictly than others?

What admonitions and comments about speech do we see elsewhere in the Scriptures?

Read:

James 1:19

James 2:12

James 4:11-12

Proverbs 10:11

Matthew 15:11

Mark 7:15

If a person were never at fault in what he or she said, what would that show about them?

James tries to impress his readers about the vital importance of speech. In doing so, he uses six pictures of the tongue. Identify these pictures.

In using these pictures, James illustrates three very specific powers of the tongue: the power to direct, the power to destroy, and the power to delight and heal. These powers can be used for good or for ill.

The Power to Direct: The Bit and the Rudder

Read:

James 3:3-4

Proverbs 18:21

The Power to Destroy: Fire

Read:

James 3:5-6

Proverbs 26:20-21

Psalm 39:1-3

The Power to Delight and Heal: The Spring and the Tree

Read:

Proverbs 18:4

Proverbs 10:11

Proverbs 13:14

Proverbs 12:18

John 6:33

What characteristics of our speech displease God?

Read:

Proverbs 15:1

Proverbs 12:22

Why do we often overlook negative speech patterns in human interaction, both in and out of the church?

Should we overlook these?

Warren Wiersbe, internationally known Bible teacher and former pastor of the Moody Church in Chicago, says that the sins of the tongue are not corrected by time, but continue to spread. What do you think about this?

What characteristics of speech please God?

Read:

Proverbs 10:19

Proverbs 17:27

Proverbs 14:29

Colossians 4:5-6

Romans 15:32

1 Corinthians 16:18

What do we learn from James' use of the examples of the fruit tree or a spring?

Read:

James 3:11-12

John 4:14

Proverbs 18:4

From where do these characteristics and powers of the tongue actually emanate?

Read:

Matthew 15:18

Psalm 141:3-4

Matthew 12:34

Proverbs 4:23

Philippians 4:8

Twelve Words That Can Change Lives and Relationships

Please

Thank you

I'm sorry

I love you

I'm praying for you

Application Question

What positive things do your friends, family, and other associates need to hear from you this week?

Close in prayer.

Review calendar.

Assign refreshments for next week.

WEEK 6

TRUE AND FALSE WISDOM

JAMES 3:13-18

Opening Prayer

Group Warm-up Question

What did God create first?

Read Proverbs 8:22-38.

Do you also see any Messianic allusions in this passage?

What is the difference between knowledge and wisdom?

Read James 3:13-18.

What quick and easy formula do we find here for being able to tell if a person is wise? (Hint: see verse 13.)

In particular, what things disqualify someone from boasting about their wisdom? (Hint: see verse 14.)

What is wrong with "wisdom" grounded in selfish ambition and jealousy? (Hint: see verse 14 again.)

What is the root of selfish ambition and jealousy? (Hint: see verse 15.)

Let's look at a few examples of the folly of man's wisdom. Read the following passages and discuss the foolishness of human wisdom evident in each situation. If possible, also contrast this with God's wisdom in each case.

Genesis 11:1-9

Genesis 12:10-20

1 Samuel 17:1-51

Acts 27:1-44

Let's look at some other characteristics of worldly wisdom. Read and comment on the following verses:

1 Corinthians 1:18-21

1 Corinthians 2:14

Romans 3:18

By contrast, let us now look at some of the characteristics of wisdom from God. Read and comment on the following verses:

Proverbs 9:10

Psalm 111:10

Job 28:28

Proverbs 1:7

Proverbs 15:33

Obviously, there is a great difference between worldly and godly wisdom. How then, do we actually get this positive and powerful wisdom from God? Read and comment on the following verses:

1 Corinthians 1:24

1 Corinthians 1:30

Colossians 2:1-4

Deuteronomy 4:4-6

2 Timothy 3:15-16

Psalm 119:97-100

James 1:5

1 John 2:27

Going back to the foundation of today's study, if we read James 3:14-16 again, we see several evidences of false wisdom in a person's life. List as many as possible and describe their negative impact:

- On individuals

- Upon those around them

Even in Christian circles, our enemy tempts us to engage in false wisdom. How can we be sure that our "zeal for God" is exactly that, and not some form of self-aggrandizement?

In James 3:13, 17-18 we see real evidences in day-to-day life of the wisdom that comes from God. List as many of these as possible and describe their impact:

- On us as individuals.

- Upon those around us.

What positive characteristics do we find in our speech when we actively seek God's wisdom?

Application Question

What can you do this week to plant peace in a relationship or situation that has been troubling you?

Close in prayer

Review calendar.

Assign refreshments for next time.

WHAT'S WRONG WITH THIS BODY?
JAMES 4:1-12

Opening Prayer

Group Warm-up Question

If you could ask God for anything, knowing that the request would be granted, what would you ask for?

James 4:1-12 is perhaps my least favorite portion of Scripture. It has always sickened me to see dissension in the body of Christ. To top this off, it presents a terrible witness to the world. When we or others engage in the type of activities described by James, we should be ashamed, penitent, and get ourselves back on track.

Some people excuse poor behavior by saying that we are "only human." David Jeremiah, in his series on James, tells a story about this in the life of Dr. Ironside, the great preacher from many years ago. As the story goes, Dr. Ironside was on his way home on a streetcar with his wife after having delivered five sermons in one day. He was feeling tired, exhausted, sorry for himself, and justified about feeling sorry for himself.

His wife asked him a question and he gave her a rude and short answer. When she admonished him for it, he told her he was justified in acting that way because of the tough day he had had delivering five sermons. She responded by saying that her day had been tougher because she had to listen to him deliver five sermons, and yet she was still able to be polite, civil, and loving toward him. He was embarrassed, asked her forgiveness, and thereafter did a much better job of acting in a manner pleasing to God.

Larry Norman wrote a song (my least-favorite song of his) addressing this problem. The first four lines of the chorus to the song, entitled *What's Wrong With This Body,* go:

What's wrong with this body?

This body is ill.

It's full of disease and it's dying.

This body needs healing.

Read James 4:1-12

What battles go on inside a person?

According to this passage, what is the root cause of fights and quarrels between people?

Read James 4:1 again in the King James Version.

Note: The Greek word for "lusts" or "desires" used here is *hedone*. *Hedone* refers to desires for pleasure. This comes from the Greek word *handano* which means "to please." This is where we get the word "hedonism," which is the belief that pleasure and the search for it is the chief aim in life.

How does this understanding of the Greek influence our understanding of this verse?

Read Psalm 133:1.

What type of relationship between believers pleases God?

Conversely, what type of interaction between His people does God abhor?

Is it possible that even a person's prayers might displease God? How so?

In James 4:4, the author refers to his readers as adulterers, an extremely negative description.

Read Jeremiah 3:1-5 and explain the import of James applying the term "adulterers" to the recipients of his letter.

Types of Disagreements or Wars

The Scriptures relate several types of disagreements that may erupt between people. Read the following verses and comment about the type of war or conflict mentioned:

James 2:1-9

James 5:1-4

James 1:19-20

James 3:13-18

James 4:11-12

Galatians 6:1-2

Ways in which Believers Have Been at War

The passage we are studying today, James 4:1-12, lists at least three negative ways in which even believers have sometimes been at war: with each other, with ourselves, and with God.

WAR WITH EACH OTHER

Read and comment on the following verses:

James 4:1

James 4:11-12

Luke 9:46-48

1 Corinthians 6:1-8

List some of the results of these kinds of problems.

Read Galatians 5:15 and comment.

WAR WITH OURSELVES

Read James 4:1-3 again and comment.

WAR WITH GOD

Read James 4:4-10 again and comment.

Commanded to Be at War

At the same time, believers must be at war with three entities: the world, the flesh, and the devil.

THE WORLD

Read and comment on the following verses:

1 John 2:15-17

Romans 12:2

THE FLESH

Read and comment on the following verses:

Romans 7:4

Romans 8:6-7

THE DEVIL

Read and comment on the following verses:

Ephesians 2:1-2

1 Timothy 3:6

What tool does our enemy use in this situation?

Read Ephesians 4:26-27

What tool does our enemy use in this instance?

In James 4:1-12, God gives us three things we must do to win the war in which we are all engaged.

Read James 4:7 again and write down the command we find.

Note: The Greek word used here for "submit" or "humble" is a military term. It means to get into your proper rank.

How does knowing the meaning of the Greek influence our understanding of this verse?

Read James 4:8 again and write down the command we see.

Note: In the Greek, the word used for "purify" means to "make chaste."

How does this relate to James 4:4 and how does it then influence our understanding of this command?

Read James 4:9-10 again and write down the command we find here.

How does God want believers to relate to one another?

Read and comment on the following verses:

James 4:11-12

1 Peter 4:8

Matthew 18:15-19

Galatians 6:1-2

Ephesians 4:1-16

Application Questions

What can you do this week to draw near to God and enhance your relationship with Him?

What can you do this week to help bring about the kind of relationship between believers that pleases God?

Close in Prayer.

Review calendar.

Assign refreshments for next time.

LONG-TERM PLANNING
JAMES 4:13-17

Opening Prayer

Group Warm-up Question

If you knew for sure that you had just three months to live, what things would you want to do?

To begin today, let's read James 4:13-17 to get an overview of the concepts we will discuss.

Read James 4:13 again.

In particular, to whom do you think James addressed verse 13?

Now read James 5:1.

James begins James 5:1 and James 4:13 with exactly the same words in Greek. This is particularly noteworthy since this phrase, translated "look here" or "come now" is used only two places in the whole of Scripture.

What is the significance of the way God uses these particular strong terms in these two very specific verses?

Read Luke 12:15-40.

What seem to have been the key problems for the man described in this parable? Please List.

In this same passage Jesus gives us the solutions to the problems that plagued this man. Please list them.

Read James 4:14.

How would you answer the question James poses in this verse?

Read the following verses to see how this concept is found elsewhere in Scripture:

Job 7:6

Job 7:7

Job 8:9

Job 9:25-26

Job 14:1-2

Psalm 102:3

In particular, let's read Psalm 90:12 in several different translations to see what we can learn from it.

What does this say about the importance of each and every day we live?

What excuse do we have for "bad hair days?"

Read James 4:15 again.

Is it bad for a believer to make long-range plans?

How should a believer approach this important aspect of life?

What problems arise when believers fail to make long-range plans? Please make a list.

Read the following verses to get a feel for the overall biblical view of planning and how we conduct our lives. As we read, let's pay particular attention to what we learn from each reference.

Proverbs 21:5

Proverbs 21:30-31

Proverbs 22:3

Proverbs 24:7

Proverbs 22:29

Colossians 3:23-24

Chuck Missler says: "The secret of a happy life is to delight in duty. Work is kind of a prayer when you're home."[1] How do you feel about this?

Read:

Psalm 40:8

Psalm 119:35

Psalm 1:2

James 4:16

What problems arise when believers make long-range plans incorrectly?

Read Proverbs 27:1.

What is worth boasting about?

Read Jeremiah 9:24.

Note: According to information presented in *Darwin on The Rocks* (with John Mackay, International Director of Creation Research, 2009, Creation Research. net), there is a great difference in the results obtained from sharing the gospel with natives in Papua, New Guinea, in two different ways. One group has been evangelized with the New Testament only. They seem subject to cults, native superstitions, back sliding, poor habits, disobedience, etc.... The other has been evangelized with the first 12 chapters of Genesis as well as the Gospel of Mark. The second group lives a consistent Christian life.

Why the difference?

Read James 4:17 again.

How does the experience of the indigenous new believers in Papua, New Guinea, directly relate to what James says in this verse?

Read the following verses and expand upon how we can know what we ought to do:

Ephesians 5:16-17

2 Timothy 3:16-17

2 Peter 2:21

Joshua 1:8

Psalm 1:1-3

What must our response be when we know what to do?

Read:

Luke 12:47-48

Proverbs 24:11-12

Proverbs 3:27-28

Romans 12:2

Note that the Greek verb used in this passage for "proving" or "knowing" God's will means to "prove by experience."

If we are to prove God's will by experience, what does this infer?

Read 1 John 2:17.

What wonderful promise do we find in this verse?

What assumptions are inherently made about the faith, trust, and hope of a person able to claim this promise?

Application Question

When we began today, we asked what you would do if you had just three months to live. However, as we see, none of us is promised that we will be alive three months, three days, or three hours from now. How does thinking about this influence the way you view your future?

Close in prayer.

Review Calendar.

Assign refreshments for next time.

THE WEALTHY WICKED

JAMES 5:1-6

Opening prayer

Group Warm-up Question

How much money does it take for someone to be considered rich in your sphere of life?

Read James 5:1-6.

To whom is this particular passage addressed?

Reading this in context, do you believe it is addressed to all rich people, or to a certain segment of that group?

Note: We need to remember that wealth is not a sin. However, it does have certain unique hazards and potential uses. Indeed, many famous and important personages in the scriptures were wealthy by human standards. This included Abraham, Job, David, Solomon, Josiah, Philemon, Joseph of Arimathea, and Lydia. Earthly wealth can be a deadly trap, or a positive tool and opportunity.

What happens to people psychologically when they consider themselves to be financially rich?

What problems were there with the wealth of those people referenced in James 5:2-6? Please list as many as you can.

Read James 5:3 again.

How does God feel about saving and planning for the future?

Read and comment on the following verses:

    2 Corinthians 12:14

    1 Timothy 5:8

Is money itself evil?

Read 1 Timothy 6:10 and comment.

To what does the love of money lead? Please list as many things as you can come up with.

What is the long term (eternal) destination of the material riches and wealth one accumulates in this life?

How do they help you on the day you die?

Read James 5:4 again.

Note: The tense of the verb "kept back" in the original Greek indicates that the workers *will never get their pay.*

What does God have to say about this?

Read and comment on the following verses:

    Deuteronomy 24:14-15

    Leviticus 19:13

    Jeremiah 22:13

Who actually "owns" all wealth?

Read Psalm 50:10-12 and comment.

What responsibilities do all believers have in regard to the assets over which they have control?

Read and comment on the following verses:

    Isaiah 33:15

    Matthew 25:14-30

    1 Corinthians 4:2

    Ephesians 5:15-16

    John 9:4

    Matthew 6:19-21

What exactly do you think God meant in these verses?

For more biblical perspective on riches, read the following verses:

Psalm 62:10

Proverbs 11:28

Proverbs 19:17

Proverbs 22:1

1 Timothy 6:17

How seriously does God regard what we do with our lives and possessions?

Read and comment on the following verses:

Romans 14:10-12

2 Corinthians 5:9-10

Revelation 20:11-15

1 Corinthians 3:1-15

Note: Read James 4:13 again. Remember that there are only two places in all of Scripture where the passage begins with these same two words.

What is the significance of the fact that this expression is used only twice and that it is used in these two places? (James 4: 13 and James 5: 4)

Read James 5:4 again.

How did the believers cited in this passage respond when oppressed in a fashion that they could not resist?

Read James 5:5 again.

In his commentary on the New Testament, Warren Wiersbe retells the story told in a magazine of an oil rich Sultan who went on a shopping spree. He purchased 19 Cadillacs®, one for each of his nineteen wives, and paid extra to have the cars made longer. He also purchased two Porsches®, six Mercedes®, a speedboat, and a truck for transporting it. In addition, he picked up sixteen refrigerators, $47,000 worth of women's luggage, two Florida grapefruit trees, two reclining chairs, and one slot machine. At the time, this cost him only $1.5 million and another $194,500 to have it delivered.

Does this seem like the luxury mentioned in James 5:5?

Do we ever indulge in meaningless and needless luxuries?

Read James 5:6 again.

This verse seems to indicate that the "wealthy wicked" have actually killed people in order to increase their wealth. Do you see this happening in the world today?

Read and comment on the following verses:

James 2:6

Amos 5:12

When we read these verses together with James 5:6, what additional light do we see shed on what the "wicked wealthy" might do?

Does this happen today?

What does God have to say about the concept of courts?

Read and comment on the following verses:

Exodus 18:21

Leviticus 19:15

Deuteronomy 19:16-21

Amos 5:12, 15

What happened when the ancient Jewish Judges and leaders did not live up to God's standards of conduct?

Read and comment on the following verses:

    Micah 3:1-12

    Micah 7:2-4

What implications does this have for any culture where this type of behavior exists?

Does this have any implications for the country in which you live?

What responsibility do God's people have in the face of conditions like this?

Read Amos 5:14-15 and comment.

In the end, what will happen with the people of Israel?

Read: Jeremiah 31:31-34

What does this mean to us in our day-to-day lives now?

How should it influence the way we act and what we say?

Application Question

What changes can you make in your habitual use of money and other assets that would be pleasing to God?

Close in prayer.

Review calendar.

Assign refreshments for next time.

THE NEGATIVE POWER OF GRUMBLING
JAMES 5:7-12

Opening Prayer

Group Warm-up Question

How can you tell if a person is telling the truth or making a promise that they will keep?

Read James 5:7-12.

What should we do as we wait for Christ's return?

Note: Greek scholars say that there are two kinds of patience. One type refers to patience in respect to persons. The other refers to patience in respect to circumstances.

Why do you think they differentiate between these two types of patience?

Which type of patience is harder to have?

Which of these types of patience should we have?

Why do you think this was likened to the work of a farmer?

Note: Israel experienced their autumn rains in October and November, followed by winter rains in December and January. This accounted for fully 75% of the year's expected precipitation. They really needed and looked forward to this rainfall.

They harvested barley in March. The main wheat harvest happened from mid-April through the end of May. In Greece, the main rain harvest came in June. In Italy, the grain harvest fell in July.

These farmers and their families depended entirely on good harvests. Their very survival depended upon this cycle.

Read Psalm 37:7 and comment.

What kind of a harvest does God want in our lives?

Read Galatians 5:22-23.

Like the farmer, what do we observe in James 5:8 that is part of this process?

Read James 5:8.

Why is it sometimes hard to wait for "God's timing"?

What is the secret to having the type of patience James tells us to have?

Read and comment on the following verses:

  Galatians 6:9

  Mark 4:26-29

Read James 5:9 again.

Why was this so important to James?

Why is it so important to us?

Read James 4:11-12 and comment.

What sometimes causes believers to grumble against one another?

What does God think about this?

Read James 5:10 again.

Why do you think James tells us to do this?

Read the following verses for more insight into this:
    Matthew 5:10-12
    2 Timothy 3:12
    Matthew 25:33-41

Matthew 22:1-7

Matthew 23:29-37

Acts 7:51-52

Hebrews 11:33-38

Read James 5:11 again.

In what ways does God help us when we must endure suffering?

James mentions the example of Job.

Read Job 2:3.

What did Job do against God to warrant the suffering he experienced?

Read Job 42:1-17.

In the end, what resulted from the suffering endured by Job? Go beyond the material as you contemplate your answer.

What lessons from Job's life can we apply to ours?

Read James 5:12 again.

What does James refer to when he speaks of oaths?

How does this relate to what is commonly called "swearing" in our culture?

Note: Oaths were verbal confirmations guaranteed by appeal to a divine witness.

Read the following verses to learn more about oaths:

Exodus 20:7

Deuteronomy 5:11

Leviticus 19:12

Numbers 30:2

Deuteronomy 23:21

Matthew 5:34-37

However, there are apparently appropriate solemn oaths. Read the following and comment:

Matthew 26:63-64

2 Corinthians 1:23

With all this background, what is the best way for us to deal with oaths and the things we promise to do? (Go back to James 5:12.)

Read and remember Matthew 12:36-37.

Application Questions

In what situation do you need God's help to have patience this coming week?

What can a believer do to be trusted when he or she makes a promise or gives their word?

Close in prayer.

Review calendar.

Assign refreshments for next time.

IT'S A TEAM EFFORT

JAMES 5:13-20

Opening prayer

Group Warm-up Question

When does the average person turn to prayer?

Read James 5:13-14.

What are we instructed to do if we are in trouble?

Why?

81

What should we do if we are happy? Why?

Read Acts 16:25.

What did Paul and Silas do in their strange circumstances?

What effect did it have upon them and those around them?

In the following verses, we learn several important things about the praise of a believer. Read these verses and list these characteristics of praise as you go through them:

    1 Corinthians 14:15

    Ephesians 5:19

    Ephesians 5:18

    Colossians 3:16

When finished, your list should include the following points:

1. A believer's praise should be intelligent and not just involve mouthing words.

2. It should come from the heart.

3. It should be motivated by the Holy Spirit.

4. It should be based upon Scripture.

Read James 5:14-15.

What should we do if we are ill? Why?

What are the church elders to do for someone who is sick?

Does this mean that everyone gets better?

Can there be a purpose in recovery or ill health? How so?

Read and comment on the following verses:

2 Timothy 4:20

Philippians 2:27

2 Corinthians 12:6-10

Read James 5:14-16.

What does sin seem to have to do with this process?

Does this mean that sin made someone ill?

Read 1 Corinthians 11:25-30.

What thoughts, attitudes, and actions had such a negative effect on some of the believers in Corinth?

Read and comment on the following verses:

James 4:5-7

James 5:16

1 John 1:9

Proverbs 28:13

Why is it important to confess our sins to each other?

What effect does this have on the one confessing, the one hearing the confession, and the body of believers in general?

What effect does it have on a person when they hear others praying for them? How does it affect you?

Why does the prayer of a righteous person seem to have such a powerful effect?

Can you think of a time when a person you considered to be righteous prayed? What effect did it have?

What extraordinary or unusual answers to prayer have you received in your life?

What can hinder a person from going through this process of assisting one another?

Read James 5:17-18.

What do we learn from the example of Elijah?

What particular characteristic did Elijah's praying have that ours should also have?

Read James 5:19-20.

How can a believer wander away from the truth?

Read and comment on the following verses:

    Hebrews 2:1

    John 17:17

What should we do if we see this happening?

How exactly are we to go about this?

Does this vary depending upon the severity of the situation?

Read and comment on the following verses:

    Matthew 18:15

    Matthew 18:16-17

    1 John 5:16-17

    1 Corinthians 5:11

    1 Peter 4:8

How do these two thoughts work together in a practical and positive fashion if we diligently put them into use?

What happens when someone does not respond positively to the formula in Matthew 18:15-17?

Read the following verses and comment on them in the context of our discussion.

    Proverbs 1:24-32

    Psalm 2: 4

What happens when someone responds positively to the formula in Mathew 18:15-17?

Read 2 Corinthians 7:10-11 and comment.

Why is such discipline necessary for the health of the body of believers?

Read and comment on the following verses.

    I Corinthians 15:33

    Galatians 5:9

As an important adjunct we should note that in today's relativistic society many find discipline and accountability difficult, even among believers. We would do well to take this a step further and examine this concept of interaction with others in the life of Jesus Christ and his associates.

Jesus himself was accused of spending time with the outcasts of society.

Read Matthew 9:8-13 to see this.

At the same time, Jesus spoke harshly to the Pharisees, the religious leaders of his day.

Read the following verses:

Matthew 3:5-8

Matthew 21:28-32

Matthew 12:33-36

Why did he do this?

Were the Pharisees held to a higher standard than those who did not claim to be arbiters of the truth and guides for others?

Read Luke 12:48.

How do we see this playing out in the following example?

Read Mark 12:1-9.

How does this relate to us today?

Who in Scripture is responsible for knowing and judging hearts?

Contemplate your answer as you read the following verses:

    I Thessalonians 2:4

    Romans 8:27

    I Corinthians 4:5

    Acts 1:24

    Acts 15:8

Reread Matthew 12:34 for a real time example of Jesus Christ engaging in this activity.

As we relate this to us today, it does not appear that we are responsible for judging people's hearts. That is God's job.

We are, however, responsible for keeping ourselves in line with the light of God's Word.

Read:

Luke 6: 44-49

Matthew 5: 12-16

And, as we see from all of the foregoing verses, we are also responsible for helping each other keep on track and in tune with the Word of God.

Question: How can we prevent this wandering away from the truth spoken of in James from happening to us?

Read and comment on the following verses:

1 Thessalonians 5:15-22

2 Timothy 3:16-17

Luke 22:32

Application Questions

What can you ask your believing and caring brothers and sisters to pray for on your behalf this week? (I suggest everyone is sure to take notes so that they can follow up on this commitment.)

What can you do this week to help another believer who needs some encouragement?

Close in prayer.

Review calendar.

Assign refreshments for next time.